Worms

by **Trudi Strain Trueit**

Reading Consultant: Nanci R. Vargus, Ed.D.

Marshall Cavendish
Benchmark
New York

Picture Words

 bird

 dirt

 flower

 hand

 leaf

rocks

 sand

 water

 worms

Some wiggle.

Some wiggle in the .

Some wiggle on a .

Some ⟿ wiggle on
a 🍃.

Some wiggle on the ▮.

Some wiggle in the .

Some wiggle on the .

Some 🪱 wiggle in a 🐦's beak.

Words to Know

beak (beek)
    a bird's mouth

wiggle (wig-uhl)
    to move quickly from side to side

Find Out More

Books

Bailey, Jill. *Worm*. Chicago, Il: Heinemann Library, 2006.

Murray, Peter. *Worms*. Chanhassen, MN: Child's World, 2005.

Parker, Steve. *Nematodes, Leeches, and Other Worms*. Minneapolis, MN: Compass Point Books, 2006.

Weber, Valerie. *Giant Tubeworms*. Milwaukee, WI: Gareth Stevens, 2005.

DVD

Way Cool Wildlife: Crazy Creepy Crawlers. Mambo Maniacs, 2006.

Web Sites

Discovery Kids: Worm World
http://yucky.discovery.com/flash/worm

University of Illinois: The Adventures of Herman the Worm
http://www.urbanext.uiuc.edu/worms

University of Michigan: Bio Kids Critter Catalog
http://www.biokids.umich.edu/critters/Annelida/

About the Author

Trudi Strain Trueit has written more than forty nonfiction books for children, from early readers to biographies to self-help books for teens. She writes fiction, too, and is the author of the popular *Julep O'Toole* series for middle grade readers. Born and raised in the Pacific Northwest, Trudi lives near Seattle, Washington with her husband. She has a B.A. in broadcast journalism. Born and raised near Seattle, Trudi still lives in the Pacific Northwest—home to the biggest earthworms in North America (they can grow up to 3 feet long)! Learn more about Trudi and her books at **www.truditrueit.com**.

About the Reading Consultant

Nanci R. Vargus, Ed.D., used to teach first grade. Now she works at the University of Indianapolis. Nanci helps young people become teachers. Nanci appreciates how worms improve the soil and help her grow strong and pretty flowers.

Marshall Cavendish Benchmark
99 White Plains Road
Tarrytown, NY 10591-5502
www.marshallcavendish.us

Library of Congress Cataloging-In-Publication Data
Trueit, Trudi Strain.
Worms / by Trudi Strain Trueit.
      p. cm. — (Benchmark rebus. Creepy critters)
Summary: "Easy to read text with rebuses explores the different places worms can be found"—Provided by publisher.
ISBN 978-0-7614-3966-0
1. Worms—Juvenile literature. I. Title.
QL386.6T78 2009
592'.3—dc22
      2008015997

Editor: Christine Florie
Publisher: Michelle Bisson
Art Director: Anahid Hamparian
Series Designer: Virginia Pope

Photo research by Connie Gardner

Rebus images provided courtesy of *Dorling Kindersley*.

Cover photo by Bill Beatty/Animals, Animals

The photographs in this book are used with permission and through the courtesy of:
Animals, Animals: p. 5 Scott W. Smith; *Photo Researchers*: p. 7 Nigel Caitlin; p. 9 Stuart Wilson; p. 11 Harry Rogers;
p. 17 Fletcher and Baylis; *Alamy*: p. 13 Derrick Alderman; *Peter Arnold*: p. 15 Joe Graham; *Getty Images*: p. 19 Ron Erwin;
p. 21 Richard Bloom.

Printed in Malaysia
1 3 5 6 4 2